INDIANS OF THE NORTHEAST WOODLANDS

INDIANS OF THE NORTHEAST WOODLANDS

BEATRICE SIEGEL

Illustrations by
William Sauts Bock

WALKER AND COMPANY ❋ **NEW YORK**

Revised edition published in the
United States of America in 1992
by Walker Publishing Company, Inc.

Published simultaneously in Canada by
Thomas Allen & Son
Canada, Limited, Markham, Ontario

Library of Congress Cataloging-in-Publication Data
Siegel, Beatrice.
Indians of the northeast woodlands / by
Beatrice Siegel ; illustrations by William Sauts Bock.
p.   cm.
Rev. & updated ed. of: Indians of the woodland : before and after the
Pilgrims. 1972.
Includes bibliographical references.
Summary: Describes the way of life of the Woodland Indians of the
Northeast before the arrival of the white man. Also discusses what
happened to these Indians and where they are today.
ISBN 0-8027-8155-1 (cloth). —
ISBN 0-8027-8157-8 (lib. bdg.)
1. Woodland Indians—Juvenile literature.   2. Algonquian Indians—
Juvenile literature.   [1. Woodland Indians.   2. Algonquian
Indians.   3. Indians of North America.]   I. Bock, William Sauts,
1939–   ill.   II. Siegel, Beatrice. Indians of the woodland before and
after the Pilgrims.
IV. Title.
E78.E2S53   1992
973'.04973—dc20   91-42785
CIP
AC

Book Design by Georg Brewer

Printed in the United States of America

2   4   6   8   10   9   7   5   3

To Sam

A Note of Thanks

I would like to express my gratitude to Ella Sekatau, ethno-historian of the Narragansett Indian Tribe, for her critical reading of the manuscript and for her editorial advice.

Contents

INDIANS
OF THE
NORTHEAST
WOODLANDS

Who Were the Indians of the Northeast Woodlands?

The Indians of the northeast woodlands lived a long time ago in the dense forests that covered eastern America. They lived there long before Europeans took over their land.

The forests at that time stretched along the Atlantic coast from Canada to Florida. They covered mountain and valley and grew down to the ocean's edge.

Scattered throughout these deep forests were lakes and rivers. Near them Indians cleared the land and built their villages. Everywhere they were surrounded by tall, thick trees of birch, pine, oak, ash, elm, chestnut, maple, and cedar. There were nut trees, fruit trees, tangled vines, and tall wild marsh grasses.

The land, fragrant with wild blossoms, was a symphony of color and movement. Animals and birds made the forests come alive, and fowl gathered in creeks and swamps. In spring and summer fish filled lakes and streams.

Living in the deep forests of what is now known as New England were tens of thousands of Indians—some historians say as many as a million—divided into large and small tribes. All of them were part of the Algonquian family of Indians. They descended from the same ancestors and spoke a variation of the Algonquian language. What kind of people made the woodlands their home? How did they get their food? How did they dress? What did children do?

This book tells about the New England tribes

before contact with Europeans and before the Pilgrims settled in Plymouth in 1620. It tells how they used plants and animals for food, clothes, and housing. It tells about family life and what they did to relax and have fun. You will also learn what happened to these tribes after white people settled on their land.

Could you live in the woodlands? Perhaps. If you were brought up to know your surroundings as you know your ABCs, then you might be able to.

◆ Why Do We Want to Know ◆ About Them?

Native Americans had a way of life that is worth studying in itself. They were the first people on this land, and now, after centuries of struggle to survive, their traditions and beliefs are being recognized for the valuable lessons they hold for us all. From their villages along the coast, the Indians of the northeast woodlands saw the Europeans approach their shores.

When the Pilgrims settled in Plymouth, they did not know how to live through the freezing winter. Many died from hunger and sickness. The Indians of the Wampanoag tribe, who lived in the area, helped the others survive the first starving years.

They let the Pilgrims live on their land.

They gave them food.

They taught them how to plant corn, fertilize the soil, and make maple sugar from the maple tree.

They taught them how to build canoes, hunt animals, find plants to eat and plants to cure sickness.

They became guides for explorers. They were fur trappers for traders.

Their narrow, winding trails became routes, then roads.

The Indians of the Northeast *knew* how to live in the wilderness. Europeans used their knowledge and skills and assistance to settle in a different world.

2

How Did They Look?

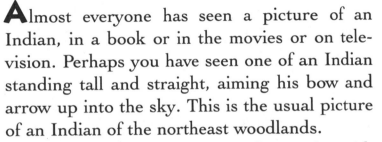

Almost everyone has seen a picture of an Indian, in a book or in the movies or on television. Perhaps you have seen one of an Indian standing tall and straight, aiming his bow and arrow up into the sky. This is the usual picture of an Indian of the northeast woodlands.

In general they were a tall people with strong, straight legs, small waists, and broad shoulders. Their eyes were dark brown, and their hair was dark brown to black and mostly straight.

When young girls combed their hair each day with a wood or bone comb, they rubbed animal fat into it to make it glossy. When very young, they wore bangs and short hair just below the ears. Not until puberty did their hairstyle change. Then they would often tie their hair back, wear it in braids over each shoulder, or arrange it in some other style of their choice.

Men had little or no hair on their faces and bodies, and they plucked out any they found.

Men often wore their long hair hanging down over their shoulders. Or they cut their hair in any way they wanted to. One style was to shave off the hair on both sides of the head and let the center section of hair grow high and hang down the back in a twist of braid.

Their red-brown skin glistened with fish or animal fat. They rubbed these oils into their skin year-round to protect them against nasty weather, insects, hot sun, and freezing cold.

◆ Why Did They Paint Their ◆ Faces and Bodies?

Everybody used paints every day to protect themselves from the elements. They used specific colors in ceremonies and wars. Men going to war painted their whole bodies and streaked their faces with red, black, white, and yellow paints in order to look fierce and frighten the enemy.

Paints could tell you how a person felt. When someone died in the family, Indians painted their faces black to show grief. A man looked sad in mulberry red but looked cheerful with a bright red band across his forehead.

Men and women used paints as cosmetics to look attractive, and they mixed paints with oil to use as lotions.

When Indians met Europeans, they were heavily painted in black, white, red, yellow, and blue bands. Red was the usual color of body paint, which led Europeans to call Indians a red-skinned people. Each color had a special significance:

Red stood for life and blood.

Yellow stood for the sun.

Black stood for death and eternal rest.

White stood for the spirit world.

Brown stood for the Earth Mother.

Green stood for plants and vegetables.

Purple stood for royalty.

Indians got pigments for their paints from the material around them. The colors red and yellow came from the mineral called ocher found in the earth. Black was made from the mineral graphite or from charcoal soot. These materials were ground into a powder in a paint cup, mixed with oils, and used to decorate the Indians' bodies and their canoes and weapons.

Colors also came from plants. For example, Indians boiled the leaves and bark of a cedar for olive green, white maple for light blue, ash bark for yellow, pine or hemlock for brown.

They got stains from berries but roots gave the more reliable colors.

◆ How Did They Dress? ◆

Native Americans dressed lightly and simply in summer and winter. Their everyday, workaday piece of clothing was the deerskin loincloth. For women it was more like a small apron, or a longer flap of the loincloth hanging down in back and front.

In cold weather they put other deerskin clothes over the loincloth.

They wore robes, long leggings, and moccasins. When the weather was freezing, they wore fur-lined robes with the fur next to their skin. Or they draped fur skins like blankets over their clothes.

They had no pockets in their clothes. They hung small pouches of snakeskin, deerskin, or weasel skin from their waists or over their shoulders. In these they carried their paints, fats, food, or tools.

Occasionally a robe was made of woven North American Indian hemp, called dogbane, or cedar bark or basswood fibers.

◆ What Did They Wear on ◆ Special Occasions?

People dressed up in decorated clothes and bright ornaments for special occasions.

A woman put on her long wraparound skirt and mantle and her decorated moccasins. She twined bright red and yellow plant fibers into her hair, and she stuck a bright bird feather into her snakeskin headband.

Around her neck she wore large pendants made of stone, bone, or shell. Or she put on a string of beads made of animal teeth. From her ears dangled copper or shell pendant earrings. She put on her makeup—red paints on her cheeks, temples, and forehead and black pigment for eye shadow around her eyes. She wore a red or saffron base paint and put markings over it.

A man dressed up in his mantle made of deerskin, moose, or bearskin. Sometimes it was made of iridescent wild turkey feathers. He slung the mantle under the right arm and clasped it over the left shoulder. In freezing weather he put a fur skin over the bare right arm.

Men, too, wore earrings as well as large pendants and beads around their necks and put on ornamental armbands and anklebands. They stuck one, two, or three feathers into their hair and hung pendants from a decorated headband.

◆ How Did They Make Their ◆ Ornaments?

They often used the bright feathers of wild birds for decoration. They got red feathers from a woodpecker, green from a mallard, orange from an oriole, brown from a thrush, and white from a heron. Or they dyed porcupine quills red or yellow or blue and sewed them on their garments. They also made embroidery of birds, flowers, and animals with colored plant fibers and porcupine quills.

Perhaps the most popular fashion was to cut fringe on skirts, mantles, moccasins, and leggings.

When they wanted to use beads, they had to make them. These beads were called wampum or, in Narragansett, *wompompeage*.

Wampum was made all year, but often women and children gathered hard-shelled clams called quahaugs during the summer and stored them. They also stored whelk and mussel shells. In stormy winter weather, when men were indoors, they made tiny flat beads from the insides of these shells.

Purple beads were made from small chips of quahaug shells. White beads were made from the inner tube or stem of the whelk shell as well as quahaugs. They carefully drilled a hole on each side of these shell pieces with a sharp pointed tool until the two holes met. Then they smoothed these little beads down on a special stone.

Wampum was valuable and had many uses. Important events were recorded in belts of wampum by arranging the beads in a special design. White belts of wampum were given as presents and peace offerings. Dark belts were sent to challenge enemies or declare war. Strings of beads were used to send messages and to identify the messenger. And wampum was used as money in trade.

◆ How Were Animal Skins ◆ Made into Clothing?

When hunters killed animals, they removed the skins with sharp stone blades or stone knives. They rolled up these skins and took them home.

Women scraped all the fat and flesh off the

tough animal skins. As they scraped these hides they softened them. Removing the hair from the skins required a separate process.

They soaked the hides in oil for a few days and then washed them. Additional oil helped make them weatherproof.

In a room heated by a good fire, women wrung out the skins and pulled and stretched them until they were soft and dry. Sometimes skins were put on a stretching frame and rubbed with a rounded stick until they were soft.

Finally the skins were smoked or "tanned" over a fire called a smudge fire.

The skins were sewn up "like a bag." The open side was placed over a funnel, under which there was a smoky fire of oak, cedar, or birch green wood. Smoking helped preserve the skins, and the smoke from different woods varied the colors from light to dark brown.

Women cut these "tanned" soft skins into moccasins, skirts, leggings, shirts, and other clothing. Using a bone needle and sinew, they sewed them together and added ornaments. Sometimes they used thin strips of leather to lace them together.

3

What Did They Eat?

The Indians ate the meat of animals all of the year. They ate deer meat, bear, beaver, moose, and even bison meat. They also ate small game: raccoon, rabbit, squirrel, muskrat, and wood-chuck.

When possible they added wild turkey, ducks, geese, grouse, partridge, and sea gulls.

Flocks of pigeons were shot down when food was scarce. They provided a special dish. Young birds were captured and fed a diet of corn and wild strawberries before they were eaten.

In spring, summer, and fall there was an abundance of other food. There were the vege-tables they planted—maize, beans, squashes, pumpkins, and melons. And there were the wild fruits and berries growing all around them.

Men and older boys brought in fish. People living near a bay had lobsters, clams, and oys-ters.

And when the first frost loosened nuts from trees, children helped their mothers gather them.

They also dug up cattail roots and ground nuts and ate eels and snakes.

Shellfishes of all species were smoked and dried and used for inland trade, often in exchange for copper and red pikestone with the Great Lakes tribes.

◆ How Did They Cook ◆ Their Food?

Women roasted, boiled, and dried their food over the open fire. They also baked food in plantain or large grape leaves over hot coals, or buried the wrapped food in hot ashes.

They kept a stew of mixed foods cooking all the time. Sometimes it was a stew of fresh meat

and vegetables flavored with nuts and berries. At other times it was a mixture of dried leached acorns, some strips of dried meat and fish. Or just a root.

People who lived near a bay made a seafood chowder, or they broiled clams and oysters over a fire.

When corn was in season, they cooked all kinds of corn dishes. Some of them we eat today.

They mixed corn with beans into succotash, and they made hominy, popcorn, and roast corn on the cob. They ground corn into cornmeal and baked corn bread and corn cakes sweetened with maple sugar or fresh strawberries.

They mashed parched kernels of corn into meal, called *nokéhick* in Narragansett, the main ingredient for a journeycake, rich and nourishing when eaten with water.

Indian warriors and hunters carried *nokéhick* in their pouches when they had to be on the trail. Often it was their only food for days.

◆ Did the Family Eat ◆ Together?

There were no rules about when a person had to eat. You ate when you were hungry.

You helped yourself to food from the stewpot

with the large wooden ladle nearby. You put the food into your own wood bowl, sat down near the fire, and ate. There were no forks but there were knives and spoons. A stick was used as a fork or they ate with their fingers.

Native Americans shared their food with neighbors and strangers. When people entered a wigwam, they were immediately offered a bowl of food. It was rude to refuse to eat.

Men and women would get up during the night and prepare a sleeping mat and food for anyone who came to their wigwam. It was a rule of hospitality observed by all tribes.

◆ How Did They Preserve ◆ Food?

When there was plenty of garden produce, and fish, meat, and nuts, women preserved whatever food they could for winter survival. April to October in Southern New England were busy months for the harvesting and preservation of food.

When corn became ripe, women set ears of corn out to dry each day in the sun. They carefully protected the corn from dampness and rain. When the corn was dried, they placed it in tightly woven storage baskets or birch bark containers. Around the baskets they wrapped strong mats and stored them in the ground below frost level. These storage holes in the ground were their barns.

Squashes, pumpkins, and melons were cut into strips and hung on racks to dry.

Meat was also cut into thin strips and dried in smoke.

Fish were hung on a rack to dry over a slow smoky fire. Or the people placed fish and shell-fish on a plank of wood to dry in the sun and wind.

Berries and nuts were air and sun dried the same way.

When snow and ice covered the earth and the people had no fresh food, they dug up their corn and beans, and they ate the dried pieces of meat, fish, and vegetables stored in baskets in storage pits. The dried food was reconstituted in hot water.

4

Why Was Hunting Important?

In northern New England Indians had to hunt to eat. When hunting was poor, people were hungry.

From when the last corn was picked in the fall until fish filled the streams in the spring, meat and stored provisions were the basic foods.

Men were the hunters. They were busy all year either hunting or preparing to hunt, sharpening stone blades, shaping arrowheads, working over a new bow, building a canoe.

The land gave them their food and they knew every part of the land. They knew every mountain and stream and winding trail. They knew the habits of animals, where they gathered, what they ate, and when they slept.

According to their religion, the land was filled with invisible spirits who lived in everything in nature. These spirits protected the people and made them feel at home in the woodlands. Before the hunt, the Indians appealed to these spirits for help. After the hunt, they thanked these spirits in special dances and ceremonies.

Indians killed only what they needed in order to live. And they used every part of an animal. Nothing was wasted. They used the skins for clothing, furs for warmth, antlers and bones for tools, tendons for cord, guts and intestines for pouches and bags.

◆ How Did They Hunt? ◆

They stalked animals. They trapped and snared them. They built enclosures and shot animals with bows and arrows or killed them with short, sharp daggers or long spears.

Usually a man would hunt alone. Sometimes, though, Indians hunted in groups of twelve, twenty, or thirty men.

◆ What Happened When ◆ a Man Went Out to Kill a Deer?

Sometimes it took a man two or three days to bring in a deer.

First he had to find one.

He looked for the deer's hoofprints. Or he tried to catch one crossing a trail. He tried to surprise one while it was feeding or while it was sleeping in the very early dawn. Sometimes he imitated the bleating sounds of a lost fawn, hoping the parents would come out into the open.

When he finally saw a deer, he followed it through the woods until he got close enough to shoot it with his bow and arrow.

◆ What Other Ways Did ◆ They Hunt Animals?

In spring and summer, men watched where deer were gathering. In the fall, after the harvest, 200 to 300 people organized drives against the deer.

Sometimes they sped in canoes up rivers or by foot along trails to the favored hunting ground.

They enclosed two to three miles of land with brush fences in the shape of a funnel or a V. One group of men drove the animals into the broad opening of the funnel, toward the narrow section. There other Indians shot them with arrows.

At night the men set snares in the enclosure

to trap animals by attaching a noose to a pegged-down sapling. Acorns were used as bait. As soon as the deer ate the acorns, the noose tightened and the sapling sprang up, catching the deer in the noose. The deer hung in the air, the noose tightened around its neck or leg or antlers. In the dawn the Indians cut the deer down and killed it.

Snares also trapped wolves, foxes, and wildcats, whose skins were used for warmth. They were not eaten, for Indians did not eat animals that fed on other animals. They only ate animals that fed on plants. The only exception were bears that fed on both plants and flesh.

◆ Did Women and Children ◆ Help?

Women and children helped by checking deer traps each day. They checked as many as forty traps set in deer paths and near freshwater springs. Unless they reached trapped animals before wolves and other animals ate them, they would find half-eaten deer or just some bones strewn about.

In the north in the fall, some families went with the men to the hunting grounds. They sometimes traveled fifty or sixty miles from their villages and stayed away two or three months. They lived in bark hunting houses, where they stored and dried the meat. Often the women helped skin, clean, and pack the meat right where the animals were killed.

Hunting families tried to get back to their villages before the heavy snows fell. There were no wagons, carts, or animals to carry them and their burdens. Men, women, and older children shouldered the heavy packs of meat. They wore snowshoes to get through the harsh, snowed-in woods. Some had sleds or drags, which were harnessed to backs and shoulders and pulled.

When families finally returned, there was great rejoicing. People feasted on the fresh supply of meat.

◆ Why Did They Use Bows ◆ and Arrows? Didn't They Have Guns?

Indians had not yet discovered the use of iron metal.

They made their tools and implements out of stone, wood, shoulder blades and other animal bones, antlers, and shells. These they patiently chipped, scraped, and shaped into needed tools.

With these tools they were able to make delicate baskets as well as sturdy canoes.

◆ How Did They Make ◆ Bows and Arrows?

They shaped a bow from a slender single piece of wood. They used the core of branches or logs from many different trees, such as ash, hickory, witch hazel, oak, beech, or rock maple. They heated the wood over a slow fire. They oiled it, polished it, and heated it again and again until they could bend it into shape.

At each end of the bow, they cut notches for the bowstrings. These were made of many twists of sinew or the tendons of an animal. Men decorated their bows with paints and carvings. When finished, a bow might stand five or six feet high, or as tall as the man who made it.

Arrows had to be straight. They were made from dry, seasoned wood; otherwise they wobbled when shot from the bows.

Indians cut down and shaped arrows from slender branches of hickory, ash, vibernum, or white oak. They also used reeds and elder tree branches. To one end of the arrowshaft they bound the split feathers that kept the arrow straight on its course. Some used vulture or wild turkey feathers. Others used crow or hawk feathers. At the other end of the arrowshaft, they inserted a stone flint arrowhead and bound it down with sinew. The arrowhead, usually triangular in shape, had a sharp point that could penetrate the skin of an animal. Often after killing an animal, hunters removed the arrow-shaft, leaving the arrowhead in the animal's body. They took the arrowheads home in the animals, removed them and fitted them with new shafts, to be used again for hunting.

5

How Did They Farm?

Women were the farmers, though men helped women break up the soil.

Women and children planted the seeds, pulled the weeds, and picked the crops.

"When the leaves of the white oak are as big as the ears of a mouse," it was time to plant corn.

Then people set to work, using a stick or a bone to break up the soil. Or they attached a large, thick shell to a stick and used it as a hoe. Sometimes they used the shoulder blade bones of a bear, moose or deer bound to wooden handles.

Every three feet, women dug holes into which they placed fertilizer and seed. They would plant seeds of beans, squashes, and pumpkins in the same hole. When the plants came up, they hoed around the plant to build up a mound in order to give the plant a sturdy base.

Women worked hard in their gardens. Good crops meant tribes could settle in one place for five months, from April to September. Then they had to move to be near game.

Children helped their mothers by pulling out the weeds. And they helped shoo away the thousands of birds that swooped down and ate the crops.

Tobacco was planted and taken care of by men.

6

How Did They Fish?

There were plenty of fish in spring, summer, and fall.

There was so much codfish in the bay that it gave Cape Cod its name.

Native Americans used nets, spears, bows and arrows, hooks, lines with sinkers, or their bare hands to catch fish.

From canoes on rivers and bays, they harpooned fish with sharp spears. Or they put nets in freshwater streams to catch bass, salmon, sturgeon, or mackerel. They swooped up saltwater mackerel and haddock in nets.

"When lightning bugs begin to appear late in June," it was time to spear salmon. Indians fished for salmon at night. Torches were used to lure the fish to the surface of the water. Then they were speared or shot with bows and arrows.

Often Indians built enclosures at the bottom of the falls of a river and on the bay to trap fish.

Even in cold, wet weather, Indians spent the night near the water to search their nets for fish. After a winter of meat and some dried nuts and corn, fish baked in hot coals were a delicious treat.

Occasionally they brought in a small whale that they harpooned from a large dugout canoe. It was cut up and sent around to the neighbors as gifts.

7

How Did They Build a Village?

A village was a cluster of wigwams built close to each other near fresh water and food. Sometimes you would see a busy village. A month later the village would disappear.

Villages were put up and taken down with the change in season. Or, if there was a disaster like sickness or drought, the village was taken apart.

Whenever a band of people decided to change its dwelling place, it moved on and set up another village.

But a village was more than its wigwams. It reflected the band of people who lived in it. Usually about one hundred people lived and worked together in a village like one very large family.

Wherever the people lived, a village took shape and became the center of work and pleasure. Everyone shared everything—good and bad. When there was food, everyone ate. When there was no food, everyone went hungry. In sickness they took care of one another, and in good times they enjoyed themselves.

They were a friendly and generous people. Anyone passing through a village was always offered food and a place to sleep.

People worked alongside one another. Men built canoes, shaped tools, prepared weapons for war or hunting. Women prepared food, made clothes, mats, and baskets, or did the farming.

A whole village turned out to clear a new field for planting. Young and old, men and women, all had their jobs. They used the slash-and-burn method, leaving the root system in the ground. While men chopped down thick trees with stone axes, women and children gathered branches and vines for burning. The elderly watched the babies.

Backbreaking work seemed lighter because it was festive. People joked and sang as they worked.

Sometimes village people just sat around to gossip and exchange the news. Often they relaxed by playing games. Men and women enjoyed races. Men played football, lacrosse, hockey, and handball. They also liked to gam-

ble. They shot dice with painted pebbles or the half-shells of nuts filled with colored clay, and they played cards with cards made of rush.

Many times during the year people gathered for special religious ceremonies, at which they thanked their Creator for his help and protection. These events often marked the change in season or the planting, ripening, and gathering of food. In the early spring there were the Maple festival, when the maple tree was tapped for its syrup, and the Planting featival, when corn seeds were planted in garden plots. In summer there was the Green Corn ceremony, when the first ears of corn were eaten. There were hunters' songs and dances in the fall and a great Thanksgiving feast at the gathering of the harvest. There were midwinter ceremonies when the countryside was covered with snow. People sang and danced at these festivals in the ancient ways handed down through the ages.

◆ What Kind of Houses ◆ Did They Have?

Wigwam is the Algonquian word for house. There were both winter and summer wigwams. The winter ones were permanent and were called longhouses. They accommodated twenty families or more. The summer house was dome-shaped and held one or two families.

The man built the frame of the house out of tall, thin saplings. For the large house he firmly set saplings into the ground about two feet apart. He set the same number of saplings opposite them. He then arched the matching pairs together and tied them with strong, narrow strips of bark, root fibers, or hemp twine.

To make the framework stronger, the man lashed more saplings across the arched saplings.

The woman took over the rest of the work. She covered the framework with overlapping pieces of bark or strong mats. Light birch bark was used in the summer. Heavy elm or walnut bark was used in the winter. Mats made of rush or cornhusks were sewn together with flat bone needles and dogbane thread. The splinter bones of a crane made fine needles.

The door of the wigwam was also a mat or a piece of bark. An opening was left at the top for smoke to escape from the indoor fire.

These bark-covered houses looked like thatched huts huddled close to one another. They were often cold, smoky, and crowded in winter and hot and stuffy in summer.

Strong tribes had palisaded villages for protection against enemy attack. These villages were enclosed by a series of closely set tree trunks about twelve feet high.

◆ How Did the Inside ◆ of the House Look?

The winter wigwam had one large room. In it families slept, cooked, ate, and worked.

Colorful woven mats of bullrushes decorated the inside walls. Hanging from the walls were baskets of all sizes and shapes made from any material at hand. There were baskets of bark, dogbane, rush, wood splints, cornhusks, tall grasses, or plant fibers. They were used like pantry shelves for storage. Women stored seeds, corn, dried meat, fish, paints, or other household items in them.

Also hanging on the walls were deer's feet, or stags' horns, or eagles' claws. These were symbols of the people's religion.

Along the sides of the walls, about twelve inches off the ground, were benches. They were made of small tree trunks lashed together and covered with mats or fur skins. People sat on them during the day and slept on them at night. Extra people slept on mats around the fire.

Each family in the wigwam had an open fire in the center of its area. Women could easily talk to one another as they worked. The fire was set in a small hollow surrounded by stones. It gave warmth and light and provided a source of heat for cooking.

Near the fire were cooking pots made of bark, wood, clay, or stone. There were large and small wood bowls. There were wood paddles and ladles, as well as mortars and pestles carved out of strong burls of wood. A birchbark pail stood nearby filled with water.

◆ Why Did They Move ◆ Around So Much?

The northern people moved around more than others. They set up homes to be close to food and fresh water.

In the spring they moved near rivers and lakes and the ocean shore to get the first run of fish to fill the waters.

In the summer they set up homes to be close to planting fields.

In the fall they moved to sheltered valleys. Or they moved to bark-covered hunting shelters to be near game.

They also changed wigwams often.

When someone in the family died and they

felt too much grief, they moved out of their house and set up another one.

When a house became too full of insects and fleas, they moved their belongings to other quarters. And when the tribe was at war, and the enemy was near the village, they deserted their homes and hid in the tall grasses of nearby swamps.

When they moved, they left the framework of the wigwam standing and took the mats and other household belongings with them.

8

How Did Children Grow and Learn?

Women owned the household and children were their responsibility until they were eight or ten years old. Then they were taken under the wing of an older male or female.

Young children ran freely around the village, loved and watched over not only by their parents but by all grown-ups. So long as there was food and shelter any place in the tribe, children were taken care of.

There were no baby-sitters. Children went wherever Mama and Papa went.

A new baby was strapped onto a cradleboard and kept close to the mother. When she worked in the garden, she hung the cradleboard on the branch of a nearby tree. When she went from one place to another, she strapped the cradleboard onto her back. This way the baby could see what was going on.

As children grew, they explored their surroundings always under the watchful eye of an elder. Sometimes they got hurt, but they learned from the experience.

In summer, young boys ran around with no clothes until ten or twelve years of age. Girls wore little loincloths. They had short hair. When they started to wear clothes, they dressed like their parents and let their hair grow long.

◆ Did They Go ◆ to School?

Indians had an effective' way of educating the young. They did it without books or schools or a written language.

Yet children learned many, many things. How did they learn? They learned by listening to their parents and other grown-ups. They learned by watching and copying the way things were done. And they learned by doing things themselves.

◆ What Did Children ◆ Learn?

Children learned the history, arts, and customs of their people. And they learned how to take care of themselves and how to be at home in the woodlands.

They found out which plants they could eat and which would make them sick. They knew that a rattlesnake might kill them and that a garter snake could become a pet. They felt how sharp a claw or bone tool could be and how hot a fire was.

They could run almost as soon as they could walk, and at the age of two they learned how to swim and later how to paddle and steer a canoe.

Children did their share of work. Older ones helped bring in food. They used sticks to kill small animals like squirrels, rabbits, and raccoons, and they helped pull in nets laden with fish.

Older boys helped their fathers. They learned to strip the bark off the white birch tree and to sew it over the frame of a canoe. They helped make arrowheads and axes and knives by learning how to chip and shape stone flint. They learned the art of working many kinds of stone.

Girls were their mothers' helpers. They cut meat into strips for drying and learned to make twine out of plant fibers. They learned to plant crops and to prepare food.

Children listened to village elders tell stories about their ancestors. At religious ceremonies they watched young men perform special dances.

They observed and were part of all the activity around them. And they were taught their skills as youths in order to pass the rituals and rites they underwent to pass from childhood to adulthood.

◆ What Games Did ◆ They Play?

They ran races. They ran and ran and ran. They ran around the village playing leapfrog and follow-the-leader. The only animal kept as a pet, a dog, ran along with them.

A thick stick was used as a bat to hit balls made of stone, wood, or animal skin. Sometimes just a pinecone or a large seed served as a ball.

They played darts with real feathers from a goose or a swan. A favorite game was spin-the-top. The top was shaped from wood, stone, or bone. They watched the top spin dizzily on a frozen pond in winter.

In summer they tried their luck at fishing in a nearby pond with a fishhook shaped from a bone. In winter they hiked on snowshoes and went sliding on icy slopes.

There were dolls made of wood, corn husks, or stuffed leather to dress in deerskin clothes, and feathers, stones, nuts, seeds, and bones to use as toys. Practice with bow and arrow was started at an early age.

Whatever children did, they tried to do well. As they grew up, they began to understand that their lives depended on the skills, endurance, and courage they were learning through games or competition.

9

What Was a Tribe?

A tribe was an independent nation with its own territory, leaders, and language or dialects.

It was made up of the bands of people in the many small villages scattered on tribal land. The people shared the land in common and were free to move about, to hunt, fish, or set up new homes.

The largest, strongest tribes were in southern New England. Some tribes, such as the Narragansett, had tens of thousands of people. Other strong tribes were the Wampanoag, the Pequot, and the Mohegan. The people of these tribes were farmers as well as hunters. This made it possible for them to stay in one place for part of the year.

The tribes of the north, such as the Abenaki, Penobscot, Passamaquoddy, and the Penacook, were hunters, wandering over the land all year in search of game.

◆ Who Was the Head ◆ of the Tribe?

He was the sachem. People did not vote for him. There were no elections. There were also women sachems.

The sachem inherited his/her role. It was handed down from father to child. If there were no children, then other members of the family could become leaders.

The sachems spoke for their tribes. They were usually able and wise and looked after the

welfare of their people. A man had to be brave in war and one of the best marksmen in the hunt. He also had to be a skilled trader and tool maker. A woman also had to be wise and skilled.

A council of elders chosen from village leaders helped the sachems make important decisions. They decided serious matters such as war and peace, alliances with other tribes, and when to call in the religious leaders, who were advisers to the sachems and councils.

There was hardly ever robbery or murder

among the people of the Northeast, but when there was, the sachem handed down the punishment, usually death or exile.

Sachems entertained all visitors with great hospitality. Strangers and friends were brought to their homes in a palisaded village, where they were generous hosts and provided food and places to sleep. This was traditional in all tribes.

On special occasions they dressed in great splendor, with beaded cap and beaded mantle. A heavy wampum belt girdled the waist. They wore ceremonial paints on their faces, as did their councillors.

People of the tribe supported the sachems by sending them a share of their hunt, their fish, and their crops. Or, if they dominated weak tribes, they collected tribute from people in the form of food, furs, and wampum.

The sachems of the four important New England tribes in early Colonial times were

Sachem	Tribe	Area
Oussamequin, or Yellow Feather, Massasoit and his son Metacomet, known as King Philip	Wampanoag	Mass.
Canonicus, his nephew Miantanimo, and his son Canonchet	Narragansett	R.I.
Sassacus	Pequot	Conn.
Uncas	Mohegan	Conn.

It was Chief Massasoit and the Wampanoag tribe who helped the Pilgrims when they landed in Plymouth.

◆ Were There Indian ◆ Wars?

There were many disputes between tribes.

Tribes went to war when their hunting grounds were invaded or to settle boundary disputes. Sometimes an insult to a leader started a battle.

Indians fought with bow and arrow, wooden and stone war club, and tomahawk. Some tribes used spears.

Battles were not very bloody. They did not fight to destroy one another. Rarely did they attack one another's villages. When they fought in the woods, they used trees as shields. When they fought in the open, they leaped and danced about to avoid being hit. A warrior would shoot his arrow at an enemy and then watch where it fell before he shot another.

A battle often stopped when a warrior was wounded or killed. His tribesmen wanted to take him home. The enemy wanted him as a prize.

There was no scalping in the early days of

intertribal warfare. No one knows for sure whether Native Americans or whites introduced scalping. It was not known to be a Native American custom before the whites arrived and began to pay for Indian scalps.

◆ What Kind of Religion ◆ Did They Have?

Indians believed in one Creator. He showed himself through the Spirit of Nature, through animals, birds, earth, children, sun, fire, and hunting.

Religion was part of daily life, for Indians had deep faith in the Creator and in their Mother Earth.

When they needed sun to ripen their crops, they appealed to the spirit of the sun. When children were ill, they appealed to the spirit that heals and gives children strength.

In times of great calamity, such as drought, flood, or disease, the religious leader, the medicine man, was called in. He was trained from childhood for his role. Sometimes he fasted and had visions. Through him the Creator showed his power.

For important religious ceremonies or dances, the medicine man dressed in the skin of an animal. He painted his face with special colors and sang and danced according to ancient custom.

While he danced, people sang out their sorrows. Some sacrificed everything they had. They threw weapons, fur hides, food, and ornaments onto the fire.

In this way they hoped to be forgiven for the evil acts they thought had brought on the terrible punishment.

10

What Were the Languages Like?

Every time you say *moccasin* you are using an Indian word. When you say *wigwam, squash, tobacco, raccoon,* and *poncho,* you are using Indian words.

Many Indian words have been adopted into our language. We have used some in this book. *Hickory, moose, succotash, hominy.* There are thousands of other Indian words as well.

Almost half the states, cities, rivers, and mountains in New England have Indian names. These place names have meanings. They describe a place so other people can find it.

Connecticut means land "on the long tidal river."

Massachusetts—"at the place of great hills."

Housatonic—"stream over the mountain."

Narragansett—"at the small, narrow point."

Nantucket—"in the midst of waters."

Pawtucket—"at the falls in the river."
Penobscot—"at the falling rocks."

◆ Were the Languages ◆ Difficult?

Like all languages, Native American languages were difficult. They had large vocabularies and definite grammars and dialects.

Since there was no written language, the spoken language did all the work. The Indians passed on to children their long history, folk stories, and traditions—all in the spoken word. Words were bold, colorful, and rich in meaning. Indians were known as good orators, for their ideas, as well as their words, were creative and poetic.

◆ Did All the Tribes Speak ◆ the Same Language?

No, they didn't. If you traveled from one tribe to another, you would hear different languages and dialects. Yet many were enough alike so that people of different tribes in New England understood one another. The languages were like different branches of one big tree. They were all part of the Algonquian family of languages. To speak to Indians from other parts of the country, hand "sign" language was used.

Here are some Native American words. They are in Narragansett.

friend	nétop
peace	aquène
sit down	máttapsh
I cannot	non ânum

Or you can count:

one	nquít
two	neèsse
three	nìsh
four	yòh
five	napànna

Then you can say:

farewell!	hawúnshech

11

How Did They Travel?

Indians traveled on foot and by canoe. A man could run a hundred miles in a single day. He could run fifty miles to deliver an urgent message and return to his village the same day.

Indians used the narrow trails that wound through the woodlands. These paths were always kept free from underbrush. They formed a belt of travel and communication between villages and tribes.

Families trudged along these paths single file when they moved from summer to winter villages. The man walked first. In his left hand he carried his bow, and over his left shoulder was his quiver of arrows. His right hand was free, ready to protect his family from attack by animals and enemies.

Women and children followed, laden down with baskets and twine or hemp bags in which were stored the family belongings.

◆ What Kind of Canoes ◆
Did They Have?

Canoes were light. They moved rapidly and quietly on freshwater streams.

The birchbark canoe was so light that people carried it over land from one river to the next. On a rough sea it looked like a "wind-driven" ship as it scudded from wave to wave.

It was made of tender young cedar saplings set close together for ribs. The ends were pulled together and tied with tough fibers or roots of trees. People sewed together sheets of birch bark and then sewed the sheets to the frame. To make it watertight, they applied pitch from pine trees to the seams.

The dugout canoe could carry thirty to forty people. It was used in sea battles or to move families. Often it carried men to hunting sites.

The dugout was made from one single, huge tree trunk. People cut down their tallest, broadest pine or chestnut tree. After removing bark and branches, they split the log and then burned it out by starting many fires down the flat center. Using large quahaug seashells and bone or stone scrapers, they scraped and charred the log, over and over, until they finally hollowed it into shape.

We still use canoes like theirs. And there are still some original Indian trails in wooded mountains of New England.

12

What Happened to the Indians of the Northeast Woodlands?

The Indians of the woodlands have almost all disappeared. Their strength and independence were broken by sickness and wars.

Native Americans living along the Atlantic coast were the first to meet white explorers and settlers. They were the first to catch their infectious diseases, such as smallpox, measles, and typhoid. They had no resistance to these diseases and no medicine with which to treat them.

Sometimes epidemics raged through their villages. Thousands and thousands died. Whole tribes were wiped out.

Indians of the Northeast were also the first to be killed in wars between Indians and whites. In two fierce wars the powerful tribes of Massachusetts, Connecticut, and Rhode Island were destroyed as fighting nations.

In 1637 there was the Pequot War. The Pequot Indians of Connecticut, under Chief

Sassacus, fought alone against the English settlers who were slowly moving onto their land. But they were no match for the English. The English used muskets and swords. Many were protected by head and chest armor. They were well organized, for their military leaders had been trained in the brutal wars of Europe.

The Indians hardly had a chance to use their bows and arrows. In one horrible act 600 Indian men, women, and children were killed when the English set fire to their palisaded village in Mystic. Flames quickly spread to all seventy wigwams. The whole village was turned into a blazing oven. Those who tried to escape were slain by the sword.

Indians did not know war could kill so many or that the English would wage war on women and children. They learned how powerful the English were.

After the Pequot War, in which most of the tribe was wiped out, English settlers quickly took over Indian land in Connecticut.

The English were increasing their rule over the lands and lives of the Indians. Colonies were springing up all over New England, pushing the Indians out. To the English the Indians were inferior to the whites. The English became the masters, treating the Indians as their subjects. They "bought up" land. They "summoned" Indian leaders to meetings. Indians were tried in English courts. Missionaries were teaching them to become Christians.

Indians saw their freedom and culture rapidly eaten away. The whites were trying to change and rule them instead of accepting them as equal and independent.

After many bloody and brutal incidents, the Indians decided to defend themselves. This led to King Philip's War in 1675. King Philip was the English name given to Metacomet, son of Oussamequin (Massasoit). This time Indians got together. Metacomet, leader of the Wampanoag, was helped by Canonchet, leader of the Narragansett, and by other tribes. The Indians now had some guns and ammunition.

The war started with a raid on the Colonial village of Swansea, Massachusetts, in June 1675. It was the beginning of a terrible, cruel struggle that lasted over a year.

Indians raided villages and ambushed colonists in fields and on roads. They completely destroyed many towns. Hundreds of English men, women, and children were killed. They were killed with guns and tomahawks or trapped in burning homes. A few became captives of the Indians.

Again the Indians were no match for the English. They were finally defeated.

In both wars Indians were hunted and rounded up. Old men, women, and children were cut down as they hid in swamps. They were captured and killed as they tried to flee to other tribes. Hundreds of captives, including the wife and nine-year-old son of Metacomet, were sold to the slave markets in the West Indies. Some women and young girls were made servants in New England homes. Some escaped to tribes in the west, north, and south.

When Canonchet was captured and about to be put to death, he said, "I like it well. I shall die before my heart is soft, before I have spoken anything unworthy of myself."

Metacomet was tracked down and finally captured in a swamp near his village on Mount Hope. He was put to death in August 1676. This brought the war to an end. And it forced Native Americans in New England to find other ways to continue their tribal life.

In both wars the Mohegan Indians, under Chief Uncas, helped the English. But in time their lands were taken and their lives changed.

Indian wars continued in Maine for many years. Finally the Abenaki, Penobscot, and

Etchemin tribes were defeated. Many fled to Canada.

Some Indians who escaped slowly drifted back to their tribal grounds. But the land that was part of their lives now belonged to the English. The life they knew no longer existed. There were no Indian villages dotting lakes and streams. English settlers, shaping a new life, excluded Indians from taking part in it. Indians had no rights, could not vote, and were denied education and jobs. They became a homeless, poor, and neglected people. For hundreds of years they were outcasts in their own land.

13

Are There Indians in New England Today?

According to the 1990 figures of the U.S. Bureau of the Census, there are now over 37,000 Native Americans in the northeastern states. Among them are descendants of the tribes that at one time lived in the dense forests. But there are also members of other tribes, such as the Micmac, Mohawk, Sioux, Cherokee, and Aleuts. Few are full-blooded Indians—Indians whose parents do not have mixed blood.

Shaped by their culture and by hundreds of years of oppression by Euro-Americans, Indians have moved into cities and villages in different ways. Some have "assimilated" and live in mainstream America. Others gather together in communities in large cities and help one another as they seek jobs or careers. Less than half the population consider reservations their only home.

Indians living in large cities may still find life

very difficult. They may be discriminated against because they are Indian or because they are dark-skinned people. Few high-paying jobs are open to them. In most large cities there are Indian centers where people can gather and use the organization's social services. In Boston the center offers a day-care facility, a soup kitchen, job training, and other services. It puts on Indian ceremonies for the community and presents theater programs written and produced by Native Americans.

◆ What Are ◆ Reservations?

Reservations are sections of land set aside—reserved—for use by an Indian tribe. For some groups these are small parcels of their original homelands.

In New England there are both federal and state reservations. On federal reservations much of the land is held under a U.S. government trusteeship, which makes it nontaxable. In addition, federal recognition and financial support improve a reservation's status and is supposed to enable it to become economically self-sufficient.

People live on reservations the way people do

in the general population. But the reservations hold a community of people who share a long and difficult history and who want to regain the right to live their own full lives. They may choose to live in the traditional way or they may try to combine their culture and the culture of the dominant outside world.

Reservations vary in size. There is a tiny one, perhaps the smallest in the country, called the Golden Hill Reservation in Trumbull, Connecticut. It is barely the size of half a city block and is home to ten people.

About three hundred Pequot Indians live on two reservations in Ledyard, Connecticut. One is the Paucatuck Eastern Pequot Reservation and the other the Mashantucket Pequot Reservation, which has become a busy center of activity. In 1991, the Mashantucket, after a long legal battle, won the right to build a gambling casino complex on their 1,800-acre reservation. They expect the casino to provide 2,000 jobs and to draw tens of thousands of tourists to the vicinity. Profits from the enterprise will be used to build housing and provide educational, health, and cultural facilities.

In Kent, Connecticut, about ten Schaghticoke Indians live on a large parklike reservation.

Descendants of the Wampanoag, the people who helped the Pilgrims in 1620, now live on parcels of their original homeland in Mashpee, on Cape Cod, Massachusetts. Standing in Mashpee township is the 300-year-old Indian Christian church, the oldest in the eastern United States. It is used as a meeting house for religious ceremonies.

Eight hundred or 900 years ago, the Wampanoag settled in Gay Head on Martha's Vineyard, an island ten miles off the coast of Massachusetts. Surrounded by the sea, the Wampanoag excelled as boatmen and fishermen, as they still do. The island is also home to Indian artists and artisans. On the high cliffs bordering the sea are Indian-owned shops and stalls that display and sell Native American artwork. The Gay Head Wampanoag have been successful in reclaiming the difficult skill of making wampum out of quahaug seashells.

In 1987, the Gay Head Indians won federal recognition as a tribe and a land claim settlement. The victory will enable them to purchase some 475 acres of private property in the area. Among the major projects planned for the new land are affordable housing, a cultural center, a museum and archive collection, and a resort complex.

A twelve-acre piece of land in Grafton, Massachusetts, belongs to the Nipmuc tribe and the Hassanamisco Reservation. Most of the Nipmuc live off the reservation where the children attend public schools with non-Indians. The Nipmuc are currently rebuilding their nation and will seek federal recognition.

The most dramatic changes in Indian life can be seen on the large reservations in Maine on which close to seventeen hundred Native Americans live.

The Passamaquoddy live on two reservations in Maine. One is in Pleasant Point, close to the most eastern section of the United States. The other is the Indian Township Reservation in Princeton.

In a 1980 land claim and money settlement, these tribes won a memorable victory: federal recognition and the money to purchase over 100,000 acres of land. With their new wealth, the Passamaquoddy have built housing and opened successful businesses. They bought huge cement factory that they sold years later for a huge profit. They own the third largest commercial blueberry farm in the United States, a mall, and some smaller businesses, one of which produces electrical equipment. Through their successful enterprises they are able to attract back to the reservation some Indians who had moved into the cities to look for work. Their success has also made the tribe a force in the state of Maine.

The Penobscot Indians, also of Maine, occupy an island in the Penobscot River called Indian Island at Old Town. They too won a land claim settlement, which gives them holdings of over 125,000 acres of land. The Maliseet in Aroostock County, Maine, also won back some of their original landholdings. Both these tribes are busy looking for industries to employ their people.

Children attend elementary school on reservations, but more than ever they go back and forth between the outside world and their tribal land. Those who graduate go on to high school and some go to college. Often there is a clash of cultures. Young people are drawn to the world they see in movies and on television. Tribal leaders, however, want them to be connected to their own history and to appreciate their own traditions. At religious ceremonies for tribal members only, children observe and learn to value their culture as a source of spiritual release. They are also helped by the works of Native American writers and scholars whose books are widely read on reservations.

Tribes are making special efforts to "breathe new life" into America's first languages. Both the Penobscot and the Passamaquoddy are restoring their languages. A recent dictionary and grammar of the Penobscot language is saving it from disappearing. Linguists have spoken up to call for the survival of Indian languages as key to the earliest history of our first citizens. In 1990 the U.S. Congress passed a law "to encourage the use of Native American languages as languages of instruction."

Success among some Indians does not mean, however, that problems have disappeared. Like most people in the United States, a few have made it and many have not. Native Americans, however, continue to have a higher rate of unemployment than other segments of the population. And, like people generally who are poor, they suffer from ill health, poor housing, and the lack of social services.

14

What Do Indians Tell Us?

Indian writers, artists, and scholars have burst upon the world with important works. In novels, poetry, and scholarly texts, they tell us how they deal with the outside world and how they live in theirs. Indian lawyers and historians publish in journals and newspapers; they take their legal claims to court. New organizations such as the Native American Rights Fund in Colorado fight for recognition of Indian rights.

We learn of Indians' unique strength, a sense of spiritual wholeness that comes from their relationship to the land where they have been for some 30,000 years. They belong to it and are part of it. In modern terms, their appreciation of the land has made them strong environmentalists, eager to protect the earth, its waters, and all life from destruction. In the words of poet Linda Hogan, a Chickasaw, they feel they are "custodians of the planet."

Indian writers such as Vine Deloria, Jr., N. Scott Momaday, and many others explain how the U.S. government, through unfair use of the law, dispossessed them of their religion, civil rights, freedom of movement, and hunting and fishing rights. The fight continues to regain these rights and to regain their land. Native Americans tell us that they are a permanent part of the United States, not only of its past but also of its future. They tell us that it takes a long time for a people to overcome eras of conquest, which brought wars and disease.

In books written for children by Native American authors, we learn of their heroes and legends from their point of view. These books, printed by Indian publishers and circulated among Indian children, are becoming available to non-Indian children.

Native Americans unite in many ways. A Pan Indian movement has grown out of a shared sense of identity. The movement provides a forum for expressing new ideas and thoughts.

Indians have also made known their feelings about Thanksgiving, the day on which Americans recall the Pilgrims' first Thanksgiving in 1620. That day has been declared "a National Day of Mourning for Native Americans." The invasion and conquest of their land by the English brought them close to destruction.

To call attention to their side of history, about 200 Native Americans from twenty-five tribes met in 1970 at Plymouth Rock in Massachusetts. Among them were Cheyenne, Cherokee, Chippewa, Sioux, Mohawk, Passamaquoddy, Wampanoag, and Narragansett. They were called together by the United American Indians of New England. While non-Indian people were celebrating the 350-year anniversary of the landing of the Pilgrims, the Indians were giving their view of that event.

They gathered at the statue of Massasoit overlooking Plymouth Rock. Some boarded the *Mayflower II*, which stands in port, and climbed its riggings. They said they were there to talk and others must listen! One tribal leader said, "We mourn the fact that our land is now occupied by a nation . . . that ignores and even rejects the people of the land." They see Plymouth Rock as a symbol of all the terrible things that have happened to them.

In September 1990, thousands of Indians representing some fifty tribes met in Minnesota to discuss immediate issues such as the desecration of Indian burial grounds and the loss of fishing rights. The long weekend of activities, organized by the American Indian Movement, included songs, dances, and traditional ceremonies.

Indians tell us that their struggles continue, whether they live on or off reservations. They want public schools and all educational facilities to teach the true facts about Native Americans. They want their children to learn their own language and history, and they want such subjects to be part of the curriculum where Native Americans live. They want equal opportunities in education, jobs, and health facilities. They want their legal rights respected.

They continue to fight to protect their land and to regain land taken from them. The victories of the Maine tribes have encouraged others to take similar steps.

All these victories, large and small, help Indians establish their rights and their power as a people.

15

Places to Visit

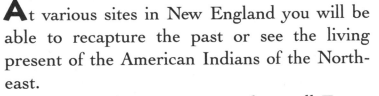

At various sites in New England you will be able to recapture the past or see the living present of the American Indians of the Northeast.

In Uncasville, Connecticut, the small Tantaquidgeon Indian Museum is under the direction of Gladys Tantaquidgeon, the ninth descendant of Chief Uncas of the Mohegan tribe. The name *Tantaquidgeon* means "fast runner" or "going along fast."

In the museum you will find displays of original tribal pieces, such as slender, polished bows, arrow tips, and stone blades. You will also see how a war club has been shaped from a single strong piece of wood and how others have ball-shaped stone heads lashed to wooden handles.

In Mystic, Connecticut, the large palisaded village of the Pequot Indians was burned to the ground in the Pequot War. Near that spot stands a statue of Captain John Mason. It is a bitter note, for Captain Mason was the English military commander who ordered the burning of the fort.

In Washington, Connecticut, the American Indian Archaeological Institute offers authentic displays and programs about the New England tribes. You can wander around an Algonquian village built on the grounds of the institute. It is made up of three wigwams, a longhouse, a rock shelter, and a garden area that is planted in season with corn, beans, and squashes in the old Indian way. In the museum are another longhouse and exhibits of artifacts that go back 10,000 years into the Indian past. Craft workshops, films, music, and dance presentations fill out the institute's varied programs.

The Narragansett tribal and community centers are in the town of Charlestown, Rhode Island. They have many ancient, traditional celebrations to which the public is invited.

In the village of Exeter, Rhode Island, you can meet and talk to members of the Narragansett tribe at the Tomaquag Indian Memorial Museum. Narragansett people teach groups of schoolchildren how to do Indian dances and make cornhusk dolls. They also let children sample foods such as johnnycakes (or journey-cakes) and succotash.

In South Kingston, Rhode Island, a large monument marks the historic site of the Great Swamp Fight in King Philip's War.

In Bristol, Rhode Island, the Haffenreffer Museum of Anthropology was built on Mount Hope. Surrounded by 370 acres of woodlands, the museum stands on a slope overlooking the broad sweep of Mount Hope Bay. Mount Hope was the summer village of Massasoit and then of his son Metacomet. Not far from that spot, Metacomet was ambushed and killed in 1676, during King Philip's War.

In the museum's education programs about Indians of the Northeast, children sit in a wigwam around a warm fire and handle replicas of the tools of the Indian people. You can eat Indian food, learn games and dances, and take part in craft programs in beadwork and feather work.

Massachusetts is rich in Indian life in unique presentations. In Plymouth, a fourteen-foot-high bronze statue of Massasoit stands on Cole's Hill, overlooking Plymouth Rock. Massasoit was the great Wampanoag sachem at the time of the Pilgrims.

Plimoth Plantation is a "living history" museum about seventeenth-century New England. A Wampanoag Indian homesite is a major exhibit. There are also a 1627 Pilgrim village and a full-scale replica of the *Mayflower*, the merchant ship that brought settlers to Plymouth in 1620.

Through these exhibits, you can experience the life of the period and the interaction of the two cultures. Children's groups are welcome to the displays, where they will see the Indians and non-Indians who work there wearing authentic dress. Slide lectures and other displays help bring these years vividly to life.

The Wampanoag and other Indians of southern New England are also the focus of the displays at the Robbins Museum of Archaeology in Middleborough, Massachusetts. Stone tools, pottery, and model villages recapture early Indian life.

A ferry can take you from Cape Cod to Gay Head on Martha's Vineyard. There you can visit the office of the Tribal Council, where someone will answer any questions you may have about the Gay Head Wampanoags.

In Maine you will be welcomed at the three large Indian reservations. It is advisable to write or phone the Tribal Councils to let them know you are coming so that they can provide a guide. They are eager to have children visit to learn what the Passamaquoddy and Penobscot have to say.

Often during the summer there are Indian celebrations called powwows at some of the villages and on reservations. You can see Indian dances and ceremonies, and eat Indian food.

Throughout New England there are other museums and hundreds of Indian names of mountains, roads, streams, lakes, rivers, caves, islands, and rocks. You will see some of these names on a road map as you travel from one place to another. These are all reminders of the culture of the people to whom all the land once belonged.

Suggested Further Reading

Ashabranner, Brent. *To Live in Two Worlds: American Indian Youth Today*. New York: Dodd, Mead and Co., 1984.

Caduto, Michael, and Joseph Bruchac. *Keepers of the Earth: Native American Stories and Environmental Activities for Children*. Golden, Colo.: Fulcrum, 1988.

Calloway, Colin G. *The Abenaki*. New York: Chelsea House Publishers, 1989.

Goller, Claudine. *Algonkian Hunters of the Eastern Woodlands*. Toronto: Grolier, 1984.

Hirschfelder, Arlene. *Happily May I Walk: American Indians and Alaska Natives Today*. New York: Charles Scribner's Sons, 1986.

Kavasch, Barrie. *Native Harvests*. New York: Vintage Books, 1979.

Lester, Joan A. *We're Still Here: Art of Indians of New England*. Boston: Children's Museum of Boston, 1987.

Rosebud Yellow Robe. *An Album of the American Indian*. New York: Franklin Watts, 1969.

Siegel, Beatrice. *The Basket Maker and the Spinner*. New York: Walker and Company, 1987.

––––––. *A New Look at the Pilgrims: Why They Came to America*. New York: Walker and Company, 1977.

Simmons, William S. *The Narragansett*. New York: Chelsea House Publishers, 1989.

Sneve, Virginia Driving Hawk. *High Elk's Treasure*. New York: Holiday House, 1972.

Whitney, Alex. *Sports and Games the Indians Gave Us*. New York: David McKay Co., 1977.

Index

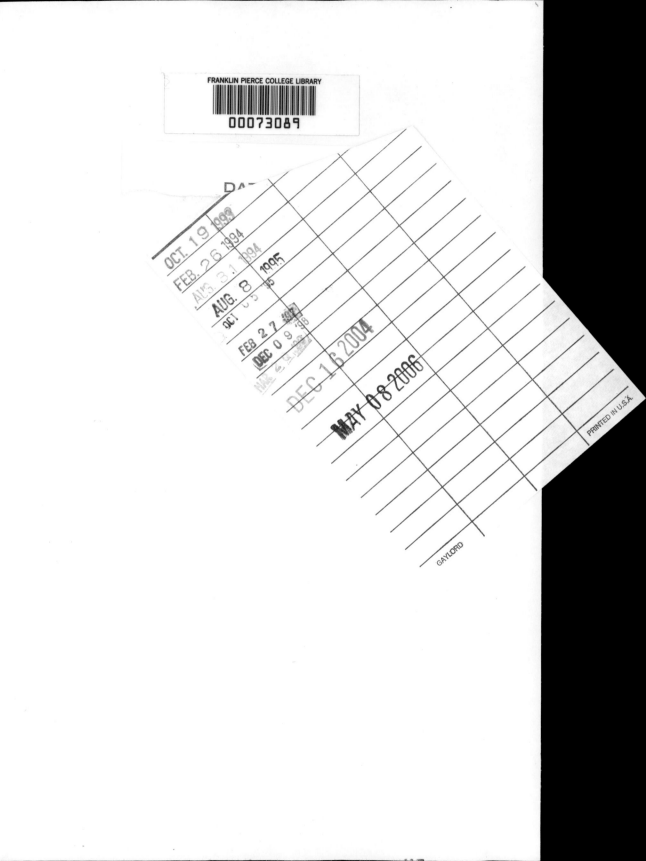